EAT YOUR ROCKS, CROC!

Dr. Glider's Advice for Troubled Animals

WRITTEN BY
JESS KEATING

ILLUSTRATED BY
PETE OSWALD

Orchard Books • New York
An Imprint of Scholastic Inc.

To Chris and Martin Kratt,
for all the adventures. —J.K.

For Anders. —P.O.

Text copyright © 2020 by Jess Keating. Illustrations copyright © 2020 by Pete Oswald • All rights reserved.
Published by Orchard Books, an imprint of Scholastic Inc., *Publishers since 1920*. ORCHARD BOOKS and design are
registered trademarks of Watts Publishing Group, Ltd., used under license. SCHOLASTIC and associated logos are
trademarks and/or registered trademarks of Scholastic Inc. • The publisher does not have any control over and does not
assume any responsibility for author or third-party websites or their content. • No part of this publication may be reproduced,
stored in a retrieval system, or transmitted in any form or by any means, electronic, mechanical, photocopying, recording,
or otherwise, without written permission of the publisher. For information regarding permission, write to Scholastic Inc.,
Attention: Permissions Department, 557 Broadway, New York, NY 10012.
Library of Congress Cataloging-in-Publication Data available
ISBN 978-1-338-23988-1 • 10 9 8 7 6 5 4 3 2 1   20 21 22 23 24 • Printed in Malaysia   108 • First edition, May 2020
Pete Oswald's illustrations were rendered digitally using gouache watercolor textures. The text type was set in
Proxima Nova. The display type was set in KG What The Teacher Wants. Book design by Brian LaRossa.

WILL De BEEST THE WILDEBEEST

MAASAI MARA, KENYA

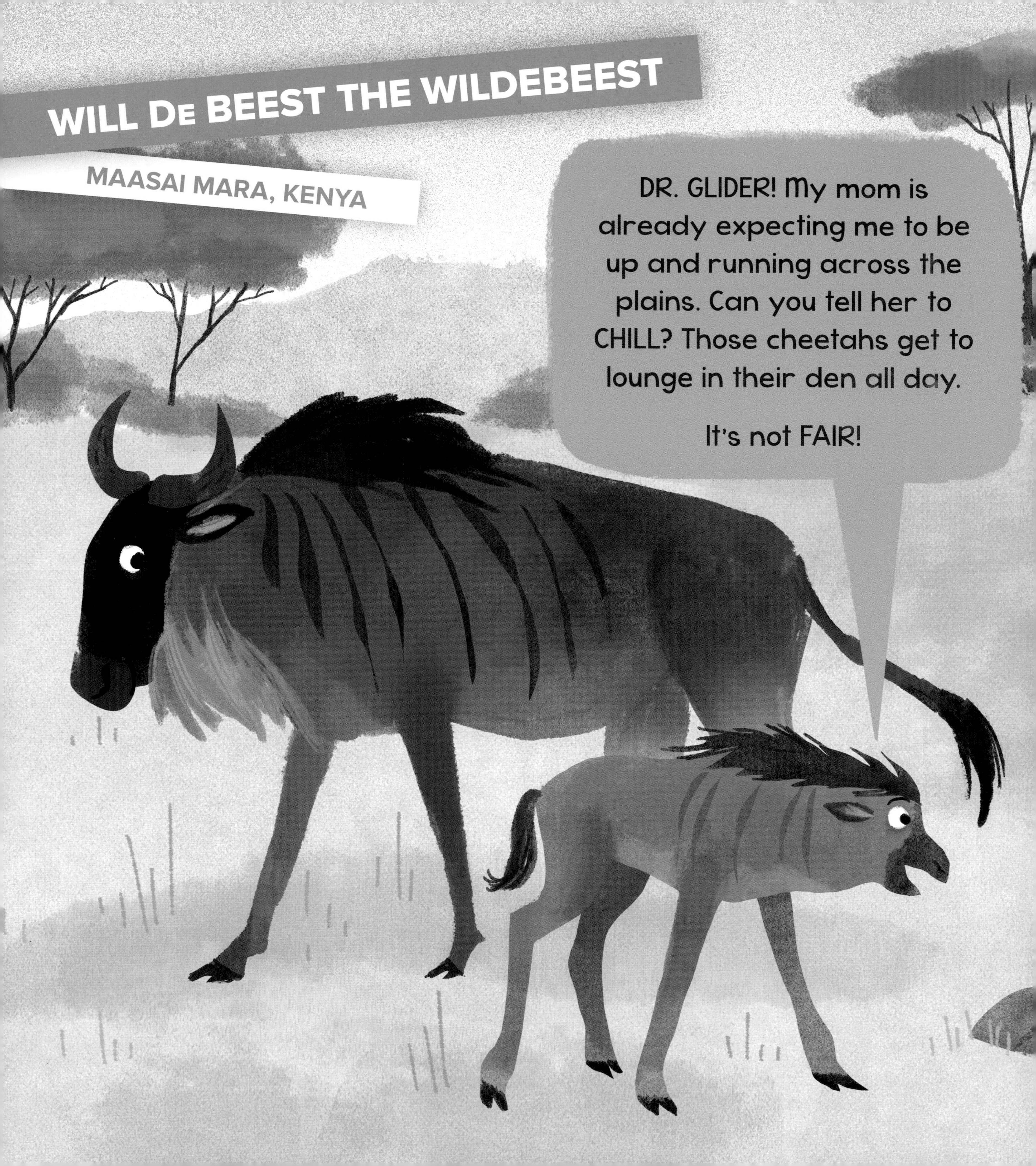

Sorry, Will, but your mom is right. The **savanna** is full of hungry animals. You want to eat breakfast, not BE breakfast, right? Get movin'!

Some creatures have all the luck. They get lots of care and attention from their parents.

These animals are known as **altricial**. Humans, rabbits, marsupials, most rodents, and some birds are altricial animals.

Other animals like wildebeest, horses, ducks, and hares are **precocial**. They are much more developed when they're born.

Precocial animals are able to move around right after they are born.

Thank goodness you're here! I've been getting HEADACHES for weeks, and I can't stay awake for my morning yoga.
HELP!
DOCTOR
GLIDER, MD
Talia, you are **nocturnal**. Skip the yoga and try some late-night stargazing instead!
TALIA TAWNY OWL
STOCKHOLM, SWEDEN

Nocturnal animals are most active at night. They have unique **adaptations** to help them survive.

Many nocturnal creatures have a reflective layer in the backs of their eyes. This **tapetum lucidum** helps them see in the dark.

> Being active at night helps me stay hidden.

> Shh! Me too!

Using the dark to hide from other animals is called **crypsis**.

Many **diurnal** animals are becoming more nocturnal because of **climate change** and human behavior. As their wild spaces shrink, being nocturnal helps them avoid humans.

AL ANGLERFISH

SOUTH CHINA SEA

I'm so glad you're here, doc! I'm STARVING! There may be plenty of fish in the sea, but they're so hard to catch. Why am I so bad at hunting?

I'm so hungry, I could faint!

Many male anglerfish don't hunt for food. Instead, they latch onto females to survive.

Once a male fish bites a female, his body fuses with hers. His internal organs wither away and become useless. He can then get his nutrients from her bloodstream!

It took scientists centuries to realize that the lumps on some female anglerfish were, in fact, male fish.

CHIN UP, AL! I've got some great news: You don't need to hunt. You just need to find the nearest girl anglerfish and BITE HER! Trust me—you won't believe what happens next.

DOCTOR GLIDER, MD

You're cramping my style, dude.

Dr. Glider, I am desperate. My brother is missing! He went out yesterday and didn't come back. Now the ants keep marching by and they look very guilty.

I think they KIDNAPPED him!

ASTRID APHID

LEUVEN, BELGIUM

Sorry, Astrid, but I spotted some ants a few trees away and I think you're right: He's been APHID-NAPPED! But don't worry, ants treat their pets very well!

LOST APHID

SMALL, GREEN, NEVER LISTENS

Aphids have a really sweet adaptation: They ooze a sugar substance called **honeydew**.

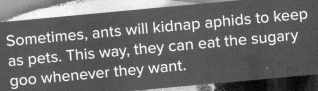

Sometimes, ants will kidnap aphids to keep as pets. This way, they can eat the sugary goo whenever they want.

The ants will protect Astrid's brother and take great care of him. (Because they want to keep their food source safe.)

When two animals benefit from a relationship like this, it's called **symbiosis**.

Hi, Doctor. There's a family of humans that lives beside my pond, and no matter how much I hide, they are always trying TO CATCH ME!

I am feeling seriously helpless.

PATRICK PLATYPUS

VICTORIA, AUSTRALIA

Oh, Patrick. You may be cute, but you are far from helpless! Why haven't you used your secret weapon on them yet? You've got **venom** up your sleeve! (Or rather, your paw.)

Male **platypuses** are equipped with a small spur on their hind legs. This spur can deliver venom when the platypus is attacked or scared.

You've probably heard of venomous reptiles and fish . . .

. . . but platypuses are one of the few venomous mammals in the world.

Platypus venom is strong enough to kill small animals, but it isn't **lethal** to humans. (It will hurt a lot, though!)

Let me out of here!

Platypuses are also **monotremes**. Monotremes are rare mammals, because they lay eggs instead of giving birth to live young.

Help me, Dr. Glider. My stomach is killing me! I eat all the same food as my family, but I'm the only one that feels sick.
WHAT'S WRONG WITH ME?
Carl, sounds to me like you need to eat more solid food. Are you eating ROCKS? A rock a day keeps the doctor away!
CARL CROCODILE
CAIRNS, AUSTRALIA

Crocodiles can't chew, so they have to eat their food in huge chunks. This can be tough on their stomachs. Solution: They swallow rocks!

Many birds, seals, sea lions, and crocodiles swallow rocks.

We help grind up the food so they can **digest** it.

BURP!

The rocks that these animals swallow to help their digestion are called **gastroliths**.

Welcome to the shallows, Dr. G! See these strange fish stuck to my belly? I can't get rid of them. I zig, they zig. I zag, they zag!

What's a shark got to do to get some alone time?

SEBASTIAN NURSE SHARK

EASTERN ATLANTIC OCEAN

Silly shark. You shouldn't be trying to outswim your belly-buddies, you should be thanking them. They're your mobile CLEANING SQUAD!

The small fish that you see stuck to shark bellies are called remoras.

I eat the **parasites** on my shark's skin!

I eat his poop!

This fancy sucker on my head lets me stick to my shark without working hard!

This "suction cup hat" is actually a modified **dorsal fin**.

Remoras can also be found on whales, rays, turtles, dugongs, large fish, and boats. Sometimes, they will even live inside the mouths of manta rays and sunfish.

Is there something in my mouth?

FREDDIE FRIGATEBIRD
HAWAII, USA
DOCTOR GLIDER, MD
I'm so glad you flew by, Doc. My family is always flying, flying, FLYING! I don't want to ruffle any feathers, but if I don't get some sleep soon, I'm going to crash!
What do I do?!
Your bird brain is well equipped for some shut-eye in the sky, Freddie. Catch some zzz's above the high seas!

Frigatebirds like Freddie are able to nap in midair while they fly. These naps are about ten seconds long, and they happen every few minutes.

Because they are expert nappers, frigatebirds can stay in the air for up to two months without landing.

Unlike us, frigatebirds don't swim.

If they had to land on water to sleep, their feathers would get waterlogged and they could drown.

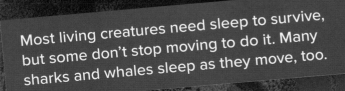

Most living creatures need sleep to survive, but some don't stop moving to do it. Many sharks and whales sleep as they move, too.

EEK! Dr. Glider! What's making these creepy sounds in the water? I hate to be a scaredy-krill, but I can hear them all day and night.

Do you think I'm being HAUNTED?

WAIL!

LOOK OUT, KRISTY! You're being HUNTED, not haunted. Whenever you hear that eerie music, just keep swimming. You know what they say: Where there's a whale, there's a way . . . TO BE EATEN!

Whales are very noisy, and make clicks, squeals, and wails to communicate. Their noises can sometimes be heard from hundreds of miles away.

Baleen whales use long plates of baleen in their mouths to filter food (like krill!) out of the water with every gulp.

Whales need to eat a lot of them every day. Some species can eat up to four tons of krill per day!

All right, everyone! Stick together!

Can I get a little personal space here?!

We are krillin' it!

GLIDER! These rats spend all day skittering up my vines and chattering in my leaves. They look very hungry and . . .

they're stressing me out!

PENELOPE PITCHER PLANT

PALAWAN, PHILIPPINES

Pitcher plants are named for their special leaves that form a pitcher-shaped trap.

This pitcher usually traps insects, which then get dissolved by the **digestive juices** inside.

Aww, nuts.

Sometimes, they can also catch bigger creatures, like rats or shrews who fall inside.

Pitcher plants aren't the only tricky plants that prey on creatures. Butterworts, bladderworts, Venus flytraps, and corkscrew plants all use different traps to catch their dinner.

We're unbe-LEAF-able!

DOCTOR
GLIDER, MD

Are you kidding me, Penelope? You don't need to be scared of them eating you. You can catch them to shut them up. Don't worry, be TRAPPY!

Yikes, Percy! Don't ask her out again—she wants to eat you for dinner. RUN FOR YOUR LIFE!

DOCTOR
GLIDER, MD

Praying mantises have varied diets.

I'll take one gecko, a hummingbird, some insects, and the head of my mate, please.

It's not known why some females eat their partners, while others don't. This behavior is called sexual cannibalism.

Uh oh.

Mantises are excellent hunters. They wait patiently and silently, but attack at lightning speed.

Their front legs have sharp barbs, and are designed to hold onto wriggling prey.

RED AND RONNIE RED FOX

ONTARIO, CANADA

You kids have found a frozen wood frog! Yes, he's alive, but I wouldn't eat him. He'll give you a case of BRAIN FREEZE that would be un-FROG-ettable!

When winter comes, many frogs nestle themselves in a cozy stream, lake, or pond to stay protected from the cold.

Wood frogs are different. They embrace the cold!

We can freeze our entire bodies for up to seven months during winter.

During this time, their hearts can even stop beating.

He's a frogsicle!

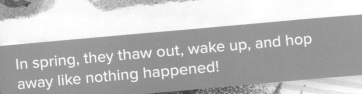

In spring, they thaw out, wake up, and hop away like nothing happened!

DAPHNE BOTTLENOSE DOLPHIN

SHARK BAY, AUSTRALIA

Thanks for swimming by, Dr. Glider!
I need help with dinner. I get cuts
and scrapes on my snout,
and it HURTS SO MUCH!

Any tips for a safer schnozz
at mealtime?

Dolphins love to use their snouts to sift through the sand for tasty fish, like sand perch.

To protect their sensitive skin from sharp coral and rocks, many dolphins have invented a brilliant solution.

By holding a sponge while they forage, they have a buffer between their nose and the seafloor.

Hold it like this.

Daphne, a simple sponge will protect that poor nose. Meals will be a lot less painful now!

Humans used to believe that they were the only species to use tools, but that was total nonsense. Many animals use tools!

DR. GLIDER! I'm going BANANAS! My termite casserole is in the oven, I've got an entire burrow to clean, eight children to feed, and **predators** to watch for.

Can you help me finally get some rest?

Meerkats are **matriarchal** animals. This means that female meerkats are in charge of the whole family!

A group of meerkats is called a mob.

Teamwork makes the dream work!

In each meerkat mob, everyone has a job. Some meerkats watch for predators. Some hunt. And some babysit the youngsters.

Baby meerkats don't work, but they are expected to learn from their elders.

Oh, my dear mama! Have you lost your meerkat marbles? You are a woman in charge! YOU run the show. Call home right now and get your family to help out. You're a queen, Myrtle—START ACTING LIKE IT!

About Dr. Sugar Glider

Dr. Sugar Glider is a sugar glider who was born and raised in eastern Australia. Her parents encouraged her love of science at a young age, and she was the only creature in her tree who learned to read and write. She studied zoology at the prestigious Oxford University (the only sugar glider in her year to do so), and enjoys climbing trees, reading, and of course, helping her fellow animals live healthy and happy lives. You can find more about her at www.jesskeating.com/drsugarglider.

Words to the Rescue

▶ **adaptation:** a process of changing over time, to better fit into one's environment

▶ **altricial:** a species in which the young require lots of care

▶ **baleen:** hard plates that hang down inside the mouths of some whales, used for filter feeding

▶ **climate change:** the global increase in temperature, affecting all life on Earth

▶ **crypsis:** an animal's ability to hide itself in its environment

▶ **digest:** the process of breaking down food and converting it to energy

▶ **digestive juices:** enzymes that aid in digestion

▶ **diurnal:** being active during the day

▶ **dorsal fin:** a singular fin on the back of a whale or shark

▶ **gastroliths:** small stones swallowed by birds, reptiles, or fish to aid digestion

▶ **honeydew:** a sugary, sticky liquid excreted by aphids (also a type of melon!)

▶ **lethal:** capable of causing death

▶ **matriarchal:** a type of community where females of the species are in charge

▶ **monotreme:** a primitive type of mammal that lays eggs and feeds their babies with milk

▶ **nocturnal:** active at night

▶ **parasite:** an organism that lives on or in another organism (called a host), getting its food at the expense of its host

▶ **platypuses:** a plural form of platypus

▶ **precocial:** a species that is born quite developed, capable of moving soon after birth

▶ **predators:** animals that survive by eating other animals

▶ **savanna:** a mixed woodland and grassland ecosystem, where the sun can reach the soil (there is no large canopy of trees to shield it)

▶ **symbiosis:** a type of relationship between organisms where both organisms benefit

▶ **tapetum lucidum:** a layer of tissue in the eye of many vertebrates (animals with backbones)

▶ **venom:** a poisonous substance produced by some organisms, typically injected by stinging or biting

Connochaetes taurinus **Blue wildebeest**

Strix aluco **Tawny owl**

Ceratias holboelli
Kroyer's deep sea anglerfish

Aphis fabae **Black bean aphid**

Ornithorhynchus anatinus **Platypus**

Crocodylus niloticus **Nile crocodile**

Ginglymostoma cirratum **Nurse shark**